WHERE THERE ARE FLOWERS AND THE MOON

Amari Dawn Pollard

FOLKWAYS PRESS, LLC

Texas, USA
www.folkwayspress.com

Where There Are Flowers and the Moon
first published in 2024

Text © Amari Dawn Pollard, 2024

Cover design by Hannah Fields

ISBN: 978-1-7362701-4-1

All rights reserved. This publication may not
be reproduced, stored in a retrieval system or
transmitted, in any form or by any means – electronic,
mechanical, photocopying, recording or otherwise,
without the prior permission of the publisher

CONTENTS

Lifetimes and Galaxies	3
Black Woman	5
Brown Sugar	7
Let Me Fix You Some Tea	8
Agoraphobe	11
I Loved Saturday Mornings	14
How We Were	16
A Pair	18
A Day of Rest	19
With Love, Your Meri Jaan	20
Birds of Paradise	21
Green Thumb	22
Comforting	23
Grandpa Frank	24
On Your Aging	26
Wishbone	28
Mothers and Their Daughters	31
Weirdo	32
Hi, Uncle Oscar. I Miss You.	34
How Is the Moon?	37
The D	40

Park Nights	42
For You	44
Spelling Bee	46
For now	48
Upon my death, please follow these instructions	49
Acknowledgements	50

WHERE THERE ARE FLOWERS AND THE MOON

For my mom, Dr. Xandria Sutherland-Pollard.
I love you to the moon and back.

LIFETIMES AND GALAXIES

Dad says we've all already met,
that our souls circle one another—
have circled one another,
here and somewhere we can't see with the limited
scope of our eyes, but our souls have reached before.
I choose to believe him,
because I enjoy the image of
me knowing you and you knowing me,
beyond this body,
beyond this time,
in a space where our minds have no recollection,
    but our beings do.
Isn't that nice?
If that, whenever we say goodbye, our words
    won't flatten us

and leave our chests heaving under the weight of
    their finality
because we'll meet again.
It may not be sometime soon, but
in another body,
in another time,
our souls will find a way to one another,
and though we may not recognize new flesh, new faces,
we'll know the same old souls.

BLACK WOMAN

I am in love with you,
Black Woman.

From the top of your toothbrush-gelled edges,
to the bottom of your strutting toes,

I want everyone to see you.

For your beauty, that persists after centuries
of being chipped away by sharpened blades
and watchful eyes that have kept you chained
to an image you never owned,

I need you.

To heal my skin that has been left dry
from a lifetime of weathering words,
being thrown around by rough-skinned hands,

and trapped on an island
comprised of weeping souls.

Just hold me, Black Woman,
and tell me when it's over—
when we have made it to paradise.
I hope Her words are true,
and that it's nice.

BROWN SUGAR

I love how your brown sugar skin
melts beneath the yellow heat. How
speckled glaze collects at the edge
of your forehead: where cane grows
from seed. It presses against your
coarse hair, like gel coaxing
rising waves back to sleep.

I imagine you taste sweet. Not actually like
the chipped away grains of sugar beet,
but the silken thick drops of
honey tapped into morning tea.

LET ME FIX YOU SOME TEA

Let me put the kettle on
and fix you some tea.

We can listen for
the whistling water and watch
the heat rise into the faded
yellow streaming in
from sleepy skies.

Let me put the kettle on
and fix you some tea.

Nothing fixes pain like
hot earl grey coating the
sides of your throat, seeping
into your stomach tissue and
spreading throughout.

LET ME FIX YOU SOME TEA

Let me put the kettle on
and fix you some tea.

I'll sweeten your day
with condense milk, let
it drip from silver spoons
like cream-painted silk.

If that won't do, let me
fix you some Horlicks, too.

Sprinkle warm milk
with powdered memories
of your mother stepping through
clouded nightmares and into
your room to soothe you with
hot malted sleep.

Or, how about I fix you some Milo.

I can go down the block
to the mom-and-pop shop and

pick you some up, with Bun
and Cheese, so you can chew on
raisins and cinnamon until
your mind goes numb with ease.

Hmm, doesn't that sound sweet?

Let me be there for you with
the swivel of my spoon and
the shake of my wrist and the
strength of my grip as I pour
happiness and tea and dreams
and Horlicks and peace and
Milo and all of me into the
emptiness of your cup.
Watch it fill up and
take a sip.

Yes, let me put the kettle on
and fix you some tea.

AGORAPHOBE

I could stay inside days
at a time and never
wonder about the sun
reaching my feet,
crawling its way up
to meet my eyes.

I see bodies cross meadows,
straps attached with their dogs
strutting in tow.

I hear basketballs kiss the rims
of rusted hoops, kids yelling
and chit chatting about their
unsuccessful alley-oops.

The birds could sing me
from bed, untwist

AMARI DAWN POLLARD

the braids from my head
and chirp me into
the clothes all set from last
night's wash. And yet,

I would still not leave.

Even though I know
beauty waits for me outside
my door, I prefer the
predictability of securing
myself between painted walls
and all this decor.

Inside is where Uncertainty
surrenders itself onto my floor,
like carpet, ready for
my feet to comfortably
explore as I sit on my
throne another night more.

AGORAPHOBE

Set in front of the TV,
I watch reruns of life.
It brings me peace
of mind, to witness
what I already know.

I LOVED SATURDAY MORNINGS:

The soft rustle of night crawling o
ut of bed beside me.

The birds serenading the sun, conjuring
Her from sleep and into the light
shadows of my bedroom.

The familiar smell of dumplings popping
in burning oil and saltfish swimming
between tender pieces of ackee
wafting toward my nose.

Bitty would sing me from my sheets, telling
me to walk toward love. So I'd slide
my ashy feet into slippers and flop
down wooden steps and

I LOVED SATURDAY MORNINGS

trudge down carpeted halls
until I saw it:

Mom turning browning circles in oil,
hot on the stove,

Dad waiting on the water,
hot to whistle for tea,

and Bri, sitting at the island,
talking about life.

I miss Saturday mornings.

HOW WE WERE

The grass grew between
my folded legs as you plaited my hair,
softly singing of Clementine and Susanna.
We lived in the sandy pages of secret gardens,
beneath loose sheets hanging from pinched corners,
as you bottled the sun in your hands.

The summers washed up at our toes. Grandma
salted fish into the heat as we played
Gin Rummy and took swigs of Ting.
We were the same, side by side,
with flowers falling from our dresses
and Mom begging us to smile into distant flashes.

You and I,
held together by the length of our shoelaces,
unaware of time—

HOW WE WERE

my spirit breathes there,
in the days of youth and ease.
Now I count my days with you.

A PAIR

Two birds
in the sky,

soaring
side by side.

That's where
I imagine
you are.

Chirping
in each other's
ear, beaks clapping
fast as you
pass me by.

A DAY OF REST

It's Sunday.
And I have
nothing
to do.

What a sweet
feeling:

to have time,
and nothing
calling you.

WITH LOVE,
YOUR MERI JAAN

The sun's reflective spots roll on the slight, dusky
hills of your cheeks; welcomed guests pour in
from sheer blinds that mingle and blend with our
bodies poking out from underneath thin sheets.

Eyes closed, you suck in the wet air,
greedily feeding on every tiny molecule
before sending carbon dioxide back into
the small space between your head and my head.

I travel with the rise and fall of your chest,
moving like Autumn, slow and measured.
I am filled with you, warmed by you,
like when walking between stiffening trees,
watching as memories of Summer fall
to the concrete and the possibilities of
blooming months wrap around me.

BIRDS OF PARADISE

Outside my window,
there are birds galore.

They are tethered together
by strings of green,
their bright orange and purple
feathers bursting from open seams.

They never chirp nor flutter
but remain gathered together
to silently whisper into
one another's ears.

I wish I could hear
what they see,
sitting outside my window.
What glory that would be.

GREEN THUMB

Flowers bloom
from the deepest cavities in your chest.
Their stems and vines wind around your veins,
extending to the tips of your limbs. Buds burst from
your fingers, shaking pollen whenever they touch—
soil is rooted in the soles of your feet. They plant seeds
whenever they meet
ground. You are,
a greenhouse:
absorbing light,
full of heat. You
are the soul
from which
everything
grows. It
all stems
from
with
in
you.

COMFORTING

There's something about
old Black hands,
with their flooded veins
raising mountains from slumped flesh,
that make me want to hold them.

To caress gentle ravines between
each new hill, silently mapping out
their destined path. To rub aged calluses
coating darkened palms, smoothing away
the wrinkles of their overworked forms.

But mostly, I want to feel the brush
of their gentle grooves as they rest
on my cheeks, for their owner's eyes
to hold mine and tell me
it's all going to be all right.

GRANDPA FRANK

Numbness gnawed the edges of your brain, then moved inward. First, he swallowed my name, because I came last and you knew me least.

I wasn't alone for long.

Soon, all the grandkids joined me in his hollow center, constricting, spitting acid onto our bodies
'til we were floating limbs and torn skin.

He got more creative after that. One day he choked down Mom's wedding ring, so Dad slid through his esophagus. Then he nibbled the years between Mom and Auntie Dawn, licking his chapped lips after he chomped on the last bit of the son who shared your face.

I always thought Grandma would be safe. Then Numbness slurped her high cheekbones and sitting thighs,

GRANDPA FRANK

so she became the plain helper who poured sweet
milk into your porridge and changed your yellow
stained sheets when you forgot how to see your
way into the pink-tiled bathroom.

When the phone rang and Mom told me
Numbness had finally finished your brain,
I didn't cry. When I saw the wax coating on your
greying skin, and unfamiliar stained faces told me
who you were, I couldn't cry. My own numbness
had eaten the parts of my brain that held your strong
jawline and your lazy smile and your easiness, smooth
as the Horlicks you brought before bedtime.

All you were was some man who used to sneak Icy Mints
into my hands before Grandma could yell, "Cha na man,
stop feeding dem children dem sweets," and sing about your
unbounded love for that darling lady we could never find.
What was her name again?
I think you called her Clementine.

ON YOUR AGING

A take on Maya Angelou's "On Aging"

When you feel me hover
Over your humming body,
Like a doctor checking his patient,
Don't think I'm trying to wake you.
I'm listening for your heart.
Stay. Please. Keep breathing!
Stay. Please don't think of leaving!
(Understanding if you need to,
Still hoping you don't have to!)

When your muscles are loose and softening
And your back won't lift you from bed,
I will only ask you one favor:
Let me help you instead.

ON YOUR AGING

When you see me watch you shaking, hunching,
Don't question and get it wrong.
Because I'm memorizing your being
And don't want to lose it when you're gone.
You're the same person you've always been,
A little more grey, a little more skin,
A lot less sight and much more slim.
But how lucky I am to still breathe you in.

WISHBONE

You saved bones for us
to break on the backs
of deep-laid wishes.
Eyes affixed on marrow,
our thumbs positioned to
conjure the perfect crack.

Can you remember the wishes
you saved in your chest?

We were told to never
say them aloud, but now—
I wish I knew what you dreamed of,
what promises you thought
bones broken would fulfill.

Were they as small as
we feel, or as big as

WISHBONE

the wish that bottles
us together still?

We must dig.

I know you don't have
much to give,

but please,

find energy,
roll up your sleeves,
and grab a shovel.

Let's go to the nearest
mound and force iron
through wrought ground,
'til we find the biggest
bone to fix all this.

We must find it
and break our wish

into existence. Please,
let this last bone save
all that we knew—
let it save you.

MOTHERS AND THEIR DAUGHTERS

Make flowers in the sand,
their hands entwined.

I am left to pick up
the petals they leave behind,

remembering how ours were
blown away in the wind.

WEIRDO

When strands of her hair fall from
borrowed shirts and chained necklaces,
I find myself staring at them for
a very long time, contemplating
whether they're really hers or mine.

Sometimes I straighten them
in the light, a thread. Imagining
I can sew them right back into
her once shaved head.

I'd transform into her stylist—
gifting her true beauty
back with each track.
Rubbing and fluffing her scalp
when done, reminding her of
how she won.

WEIRDO

She won.

Only, I am not a hairdresser,
and her head is no longer there.
So instead, I grab a plastic bag
and place the strands inside,
zipping it tight and shaking it twice
to ensure there's no escape.

Death has made me
the person who keeps a lock
of hair and thinks it's normal

If I find another one,
I'll do it all again.

HI, UNCLE OSCAR.
I MISS YOU.

One grandfather neglected me.
The other couldn't remember me.
And then there was you.

Neither grandfather, nor father.
Not blood, not wholly kin.
But perhaps something sweeter
within the branches of our
weathered familial ties:
My Uncle Oscar.

Always there.

At the table in the room
under the sun, you are
positioned perfectly to receive all

HI, UNCLE OSCAR. I MISS YOU.

conversation whirling around.
Ready to jump at the first
hint of a debate stirring
at the center of us all
gathered there.

Steadily behind the stripping
wheel, your foot pressed coolly
on the gas. Never to go beyond
65 while listening to low jazz,
or the brittle voices of BBC
coaxing us toward tennis.

Handing me a plaque,
your gentle words carved
in glass. Honoring my life
by looking back,
sending me forward.

Today, I glance upon tokens
of what was, wishing I had
stayed with you longer.

AMARI DAWN POLLARD

You are still. But you're no
longer here. Your eyes scan
my face, trying to place where
our ties start and end. Neither
known, nor familiar.
Somewhat strange perhaps.
You're always there.
Just somewhere far away,
sitting comfortably
in long-gone days.

HOW IS THE MOON?

I thought we'd reach
the moon together,

but you had to go—
too soon.

So tell me.

Do her rocks float
away from her center
to clear pathways for
your dancing feet?

Are the crevices where
water and dust meet
pristine enough to
drink from?

AMARI DAWN POLLARD

Please tell me.

I wish we could talk
about her,

about your life, there—
how far away it is.

Between us

there are oceans
and stars
and lightyears,

and yet, it feels
like you were
next to me
just yesterday.

I wish I could learn
about the moon,

HOW IS THE MOON?

with you.

But since you can't return,
and I can't find my way through

the oceans
and stars
and lightyears
between us,

I'll explore all
the places on earth
you never got to.
And then, when
it's my turn to meet
you in the sky,

I can tell you tales
from my travels.

And you can tell me,
about the moon.

THE D

Moving between tiled walls and rusting tracks,
we stop in caved out spaces of mostly silent life.

A couple, dressed in baggy wear, dances to unheard
melodies as their giddy daughter sits with her legs
swinging on a sagging bench at 42nd Street.

Carry me. Carry me away on subway seats.

A man leans against a pole on 34th,
his head hanging low, resting on the ripped cotton of
his shabby shirt. People walk briskly behind him with
scrunched faces doing their best not to get too close.

Carry me. Carry me away on subway seats.

A girl, with a slight frame, covers her face with
the worn pages hiding between the blue binding of

THE D

Breakfast at Tiffany's. I imagine she reads, "I don't
want to own anything until I find a place where
me and things go together."

Carry me. Carry me away on subway seats.

The doors open to West 4th Street, welcoming
in the sweet melancholy rhythm of Bach's Cello Suite
No. 1 in G Major echoing from the frayed bow of a man
with his eyes closed as he sways beneath his fading suit.

Some days, when life feels long and overwhelms me, I
    imagine
going beyond my usual stop, staying perched in my corner
seat with soundless headphones keeping me company.
Traveling to some unknown place, where I stay until the
train picks me back up and carries me away.

PARK NIGHTS

The soft sound of fading keys filled the spaces
in between loose feet hitting concrete,
and bodies moving through paths of broken trees.
He swayed, his eyes closed as he leaned
into the notes ringing from nimble fingers.
She swayed, her eyes closed as she danced
into the notes floating, smooth staccato lingering.
Her arms moved in time with the thoughtless wind,
careless and unaware of the crowd growing within
the opening. And there I was, drawn to the sound of
effervescent noise. So, I sat there, on a sagging bench
with fraying strands, watching people passing
with gentle smiles, tenderly whispering words
unheard. Afraid to move, I stayed, a slave
chained by a dominant force trapped
against her will. Life circled around me
and through me, one fluid note lending meaning
to the feelings that left streaks of dried salt

PARK NIGHTS

on my cheeks. There, in Washington Square Park,
as the sun bowed and the
stars started to poke out,
I found Clair de Lune.

FOR YOU

A take on Velma Pollard's "With Thanks"

For you,
I would find some eloquent way
to say we loved somewhere
between Autumn's dewy breath
and Spring's joyful cries,
blending the clouds as our awe drove
Helios's chariot across the waking sky.

Somewhere between the virtue
of my borrowed youth
and greying soul, we touched—
designing amaryllis beneath laced toes.
Somewhere between spinning around and turning back,
you stepped inside me, untangling delicate veins.
We were Summer Solstice: burning,
                                    burning.

FOR YOU

So as delta years caress my waning bones,
I look to forever within narrow days,
running warm between my wrinkled fingers.
Remembering who we were
and how we loved.

SPELLING BEE

Joy can feel hard to find.
Almost as impossible as
getting close enough to a hive
to see the honey dripping inside
without getting stung.

Yet, every day, we open the door
together and try to reach for
the honeycomb once more.

Even when the bees come
and we're forced to run
in retreat, our chuckles
manage to meet in
the center of our bellies.
And although tired
in sound, they fill
our mouths with
the sweetest taste.

SPELLING BEE

With you, I could chase
after endless hives
lining roofs for miles outside,
swelling underneath
the layered heat.

Perhaps, one day, we'll
finally reach. Only to find
the queen opening her gate,
where she waits with our
crowns between humming
legs. As though she knew,
we were always meant to
be part of her crew.

FOR NOW

If you don't hear from
me for a while, just
know I went
somewhere quiet.

UPON MY DEATH, PLEASE FOLLOW THESE INSTRUCTIONS:

Take me in my ashen form to the
edge of Ireland. Walk me into Doolin and
stop by Fisherman's Rest; tell Danny you
brought an old friend. He'll point you in the
right direction, due west, where the ocean's
lips kiss aging rock. Lay me on top of the
foaming sea and watch me drift off.
Then take a seat, lift your head toward
greying sky, close your eyes, and breathe in.
If you feel how I felt when I first met this place,
then you are at peace, and know that so am I.

ACKNOWLEDGEMENTS

I write about love because it has surrounded me my whole life. I've been lucky enough to experience people who water and tend to me with the desire to see me grow and ask for nothing in return. To those who have loved me, this poetry collection would not exist without you. You have filled my life with warmth and joy and given me the space to make sense of the world through words. This collection is just as much yours as it is mine. Thank you.

Thank you to my publisher, Hannah Fields, for accepting my poem into "We Are Not Shadows" and beginning a wonderful working relationship that brought us to this collection. It means the world to me that you believed in my work.

To my first editor, Grandma Pollard, you gave me a map for a creative, professional life and constantly encouraged me while I found my way.

ACKNOWLEDGEMENTS

To Coach Rowe, thank you for introducing me to lacrosse and setting me on a path that led to many writing and hosting opportunities. To the Le Moyne Creative Writing Program, these poems would not have been written if not for your workshops. To all my mentors, especially Leslie and Michael Streissguth, thank you for seeing something in me from the start.

To my friends—particularly Janae, Christolin, Kia, Rachel, Zari, Tari, and Omolade—thank you for carrying me through a lot and gassing me up the whole way. To my non-blood aunties, uncles, and cousins, you are blood and have contributed deeply to my life. To the Pamulas and Varghises, thank you for welcoming me as if I were your own.

To the Canadian and New Jersey Pollards, thank you for always showing up. To the Sutherlands, thank you for the love and fun you bring—especially Grandma Ivy, who refuses to slow down at 103.

To Auntie Dawn and Uncle Oscar, our family unit was so tight because of you. Thank you for helping to raise us.

To Bri and Dad, life looks much different for us now, but I'm glad we can slowly figure it out together. With Mom, we built a strong foundation, and I believe she sent KJ so that we wouldn't feel too unbalanced moving forward. I love you all so much.

To my husband Ashish, I am so happy we found our way to each other. I always knew I had love, but you have shown me what it means to give unconditionally to a partner. I will spend my life walking beside you, making sure you can always feel my love.

To mom, thank you for always giving me my flowers and showing me what is possible when you reach for the moon. I wish we had more time on earth than the 27 years we got, but I am so grateful for every moment together. I feel you in everything I do and hope you are watching from the moon, content, knowing that I am okay because of you. I love you to the moon and back.

www.ingramcontent.com/pod-product-compliance
Lightning Source LLC
Chambersburg PA
CBHW030536080526
44585CB00014B/962